Changing Weather

by Margie Burton, Cathy French, and Tammy Jones

Look at me!
Here I am playing in the snow.
I like to play in the snow.
I like to make a snowman.

Look at me!
Here I am playing outside.
I like to play in the sun.

5

Look at us!
Here we are playing in the rain.
We like to play in the rain.
We put on our raincoats to play in the rain.

Look at me!
Here I am playing outside.
I like to play outside
when it is windy.
I can fly my kite.

It is very hard to see when there is fog.

Here I am looking outside.
I can see big, dark clouds.
I can see lightning, too.

I stay inside and play when
a big storm comes.
I like to see the storm, but I
do not like to play in the storm.

15

I like all kinds of weather.